Let Me Scream

By Madison Farraway

Madison Farraway

Let Me Scream
Copyright © 2024

All rights reserved

No part of this book may be reproduced, distributed, or transmitted in any form or by any means, including electronic, mechanical, photocopying, recording, or otherwise, without the author's prior written consent.

Disclaimer:
This book contains explicit, mature content and language.

ISBN: 978-1-7382816-3-3

Madison Farraway
Ontario, Canada

Let Me Scream

I am not a poet or an author,

but I needed to let it out, I wanted to cut the nerves out of my body and hand them to you on a gold platter, because it hurt so bad. Let me scream after years of being silenced.

Let this be a reminder to use your voice, let yourself be heard, even when it hurts.
Let yourself scream, let it speak the words you can't.

- *Thank You all*
   Madison Farraway

Madison Farraway

Contents

The symphony of pain & passion….. 5

Love, desire, heartbreak—are intertwined. How passion fuels both growth and suffering, revealing the dual nature of human experience where beauty and pain coexist.

The weight of Desire and despair…..38

The tension between longing and hopelessness, and how unfulfilled desires can lead to emotional pain.

The silence of clarity in chaos………86

Understanding and self-awareness amidst life's confusion and turmoil. Highlighting how clarity can emerge from inner chaos, offering insight and growth despite all of the uncertainty.

A Symphony Of Pain & Passion

Chapter One

Passion and pain are two sides of the same coin, inseparable in their intensity. Passion ignites the soul, driving me to love deeply, dream boldly, and live fully. Yet, with its fire comes the risk of pain—the ache of loss, the sting of betrayal, and the sorrow of unfulfilled longing. Together, they create a tapestry of raw emotion, where beauty and heartbreak coexist.

Madison Farraway

My dependency of you grew,
I disregarded my boundaries that once were,
eventually losing sight of them completely.
My room started to get messy,
I started to get messy,
I started to lose myself.
I grew to hate myself so much,
that hating you became the easier thing to blame.

Let Me Scream

I thought if I hated you, maybe you'd hate me too.
Did my tears, my sleepless nights, our restless
fights, alter your image of me?

I thought if I let the hate grow, maybe it would make
you love me. Maybe then, you'd finally see—
the pain you were causing,
but the silence that grew between us, started hiding
everything we had built along the way.

Madison Farraway

She watched as her hobbies slowly started to fade, the things that once filled her heart slowly drifted away. She watched herself outgrow the things she thought she'd love for a lifetime.
The things that used to define her, now slipping through her fingers.
You watched her lose herself, abandoning the parts that she loved, but coincidently were the parts you hated. She had you, and that should have been enough right?

- *But it wasn't*

Let Me Scream

You embedded yourself into my veins,
draining the parts of me that had yet to take form;
taking what you could,
and leaving me with nothing.

Madison Farraway

Emotional Distance

I choked on my words,
trying to cough up whatever was left,
my throat started to grow dry.
The silence became symbolic; a loud testament to
the growing emotional distance, until eventually the
silence had said everything that needed to be said.

- *There was no saving us*

Let Me Scream

Lust

I confused your lust with love.
Your hands brush my face,
and your gaze lingered in my eyes.

To be wanted so deeply, to feel so cherished—
it's the vein of my existence, and consumes me
completely.

I thought it was love, I became lost in it. You
worshiped the parts of me I despised, how could I
not.

Madison Farraway

The weight of your dismissal consumed me,
swallowing every memory, every thought, until
every part of us that was or could have been became
blurry. The silence grew, and my thoughts became
louder, the need to be needed from you faded.

Day bled into night,
and the pain of your absence settled in—
a heavy reminder that lingered,
forever leaving a space between us.

   - *A void that no amount of love could ever fill*

Let Me Scream

Love, there was so much of it,
it felt fake, I hated it.
In the glimmer of my watering eyes that you loved,
there layed a reflection; stripping me of whatever I
had left of my adolescence,
you did all of this in the name of love, and I let you.
I watched the parts that once understood boundaries
faded away with every exhale.

Madison Farraway

I gave you every piece of me,
until there was nothing left to give.

- *You left me empty*

Let Me Scream

I grow and I shrink,
I grow a little more when the days get longer,
and shrink when my days get shorter.
You carved a hole within me, and replaced it with
doubt. All that's left is the hollow space, where once
there was trust. Now I sit here relentlessly in search
of the pieces of myself I gave away in hopes of
finding something whole again.

Madison Farraway

Drifting

Our conversations turned into arguments,
I hated it more than I hated you.
I wanted to escape, but I couldn't let go.
The silence grew; a reminder of how far we'd
drifted—the space between us growing wider,
until I no longer knew where you ended,
or I began.

Let Me Scream

Savering the bitter taste of stale smoke,
filling that restless void that lives within.
leaving a hollow shell of the person you once were,
and the person you could be, laying restless, and
cold. One day, this be history,
and eventually, *history will be forgotten.*

Madison Farraway

You took that blade,
shaved me down to the bone,
until I was someone you could love.

> - *You caved and molded me into someone you could love until I was unrecognizable*

Let Me Scream

I needed you.
I crumble and I fall,
screaming loud enough to burn holes in the insides
of my throat, I needed you.
I needed to know you were there, that you'd hold me
when I had my first heartache,
not be the reason I needed to be held.
Tears falling from my cheeks, my throat dry.
Maybe you couldn't understand me.
Was I not loud enough for you?
Did my words fall silent in the chaos of your own?
Why didn't you see me?
I needed you to carry me when I was too weak to
walk. Maybe—just maybe—you're just a person
whose heart was broken by the same broken home,
the same broken bottles from your childhood that
broke mine too.

Madison Farraway

I started to grieve,
my days blended together.
I longed for the person I slowly watched slip
through the tips of my fingers.
I started to grieve.
I held onto you, gave you a home within,
somewhere to hold you close,
locked you in, swore I'd never lose you.
You carved your name into my skin,
until you claimed me as your own.

   - *Addiction*

Let Me Scream

I grieve, I fear, I lost you.
your name, your blood carved into my skin
I choked on that bottle of whiskey,
the one you shoved so violently into my personal
space I let you in, and I cried,
and only when you were gone did I begin to mourn
the ghost of you that wasn't really gone.

Madison Farraway

I was starving,
waiting for you to come along to give me an inch,
I needed to feel, I'd give you my all, hoping I
wouldn't fall. But I always did,
leaving me emptier than before,
but maybe feeling something was better than
nothing at all.

Let Me Scream

Every day feels like an entire lifetime.
You stripped me of who I was and who I could have
become. Now, I'm left a ghost—
the remnants of the person I once was
and *the person I could have been, had you been
there.*

Madison Farraway

I don't think you ever needed me,
I think you just needed to feel needed,
and I was convenient for you,
a momentary fix to fill that emptiness.

I was never truly wanted,
Just a placeholder in your world,
a role I played until you no longer needed it.

Pieces of you

It's a pain that lingers in silence,
a wound I try to ignore, but I refuse to let it heal.
A constant reminder that something was lost,
that something was once whole, but is now broken.

Madison Farraway

Then she said, "I love you,"
she meant she loved their nightly conversations,
the privilege of hearing his laugh,
the scent of him,
the feel of his touch,

Her love for him grew in the little things—
like when he'd let her have the last cookie,
or ask if she needed anything,
when all she ever really needed was him.
When she cried, he'd open the tailgate,
and cry with her.
Listening, making her feel like home—
a feeling she never truly knew before.
He held her, loved her,
and every moment they shared felt like a gift,
a privilege couldn't be traded for the world.

Let Me Scream

His deepest scars were carved by those he trusted to hold the knife, the memory embedded in his mind like a hard drive and undoing it felt like trying to remove something that was meant to stay.

Each moment, each wound, a permanent imprint that no amount of time or healing could undo. The weight of pain settled within him, forever leaving a void, serving as a reminder that trust could be both a gift and a curse, and the people he had given it to were the ones who broke him most.

- *Trust*

Madison Farraway

I grew angry and bitter.
I hated that I lost that spark I had once carried,
the one that would light my way when I couldn't
find it myself.
That flame dimmed, and with it, so did I.
I hated who I became without you,
so much that I started to resent you too.
You held the match, the flame that once set me
alight, but you let it go out, watched me starve for
warmth. I pulled away, I molded myself into a shape
you could love, forgetting who I was in the process,
leaving the rest of the pieces behind.

Let Me Scream

There was so much potential—that was the problem.
The walls that held me back, but the promise of
what could be kept me. Dried up tears, sleepless
nights lingering in every corner,
they became part of the air I breathed.
I needed it in my veins,
I needed to prove to myself that it could be fixed,
learning how to walk through the doors of a home I
never chose and learning how to walk away,
knowing you would always be there.

- *Letting go*

Madison Farraway

When it's good, it's good—A rush of light, but when the day turns to night and the dark begins to creep, the world grows cold.
I've spoken, reached, and hoped for change,
for something real, for something true,
but when the silence cuts again, I'm left alone, with none but you.
The highs are high, the lows are deep, I stand on cliffs, unsure to fall, you reach, you pull me close again, but in between, I feel so small. I've carried words, I've carried weight, I've tried to bridge what seems so wide, it's fleeting, I disappear, lost in the quiet of your space. I wonder if we'll find a way to build a love that doesn't break, or if this ride will end someday, with hearts too bruised to stay awake. I'm not too much, but if the silence wears me down, I'll learn to live where I best know. .

Let Me Scream

You can't love someone into loving you the way you need. You can't force them to be the person you need them to be. You can't keep emptying your glass to fill theirs. Eventually you'll have nothing left to give.

- *A ghost of a soul you once were and could have been*

Madison Farraway

They didn't care that they were only getting a fraction of what they deserved, because that fraction was you, *even if it ended up breaking them.*

Let Me Scream

I lingered in the empty spaces,
waiting for the echoes of something that never was.
The light that once lingered dimmed,
and I found myself searching for warmth in the
shadows, grasping for something that no longer
touched me.

Madison Farraway

The love you gave was like a half-empty glass—

You filled it when you could, but I was always thirsty, always waiting for more.

And each time I reached, I only grasped the air. I built walls to protect myself from the void, from the unspoken space between us. I learned to be strong, to fill my own heart with the love you couldn't give. But even now, Even when I've grown, There's still a part of me that wonders—Did you see me? Did you ever feel me? Or was I just a name, an obligation, a thing that faded in the background of your empty days? I've learned to live without you, but the ache remains—the ghost of your absence, still lingering in the corners of my mind, *a reminder of all the love that was never truly mine to hold.*

Let Me Scream

I stopped sleeping
and my thoughts began to consume me.
I waited, hoping you would come and hold me when
I needed it most. I stopped sleeping, afraid I might
miss it—if you happened to.

Madison Farraway

Those tears flooded the bathroom floor,
I stumbled around, searching for a way to heal
the wound deeply embedded within.
I hoped to fill the void, but it never seemed enough.

Hoping, maybe just maybe,
You'd notice the salted tears running down my
cheeks. I poured that bottle down my throat until I
couldn't feel, and still, I hoped you'd see.

I needed you to hear me,
I needed to know you were there,
I needed you to understand—
This was my silent cry for help.

Let Me Scream

She grieves a life that was short lived
and with tears staining her cheeks,
she lets grief take the pen from her hands,
rewriting her story,
leaving her to read a version she never truly wanted.

- *How grief shaped you*

Madison Farraway

The weight of Desire and despair

Chapter Two

Where emotions intertwine like the notes of a haunting symphony, weaving a story of love, longing, and heartbreak. It is a place where passion burns brightly, yet leaves behind the ache of unfulfilled desires. Through vivid imagery and raw vulnerability, the poems capture the dual nature of love—its power to uplift and devastate, to heal and wound.

Let Me Scream

She was an open book written in a language
he'd never understand.
She'd carve a path of unhappiness,
leaving the same old routines to be relieved over and
over. She'd cry, and he'd pout, she'd remold herself
into someone he might one day understand,
she'd shrink, fold, and crumble herself into someone
who could be loved,
Someone who could be understood,
Somcone who could be heard.

Madison Farraway

I grew to learn you—
your footsteps,
your breath,
the sound of doors opening and closing.
I locked myself in the same room,
eyes shut tight, hoping, just hoping,
that one day we would rise above this.
Hoping that one day,
you would see the damage being done.
I'm not naive—I had faith in you, faith in us.

Let Me Scream

It's strange, how silence can feel so loud, how a
room that once hummed with your laughter
how it echoes with absence. The space you filled has
hollowed, and my heart tries to keep up,
but it's always a step behind. I didn't know how
deeply I could miss you until you weren't here to
miss anymore.

- *A road that loops back on itself, every corner
  filled with memories that feel both a little
  familiar and foreign*

Madison Farraway

love doesn't end when a person leaves, that loss, though heavy, doesn't erase what was. You're gone, but you still live, in the spaces between the words, in the quiet moments, in the things I wish I could say but never will. And maybe that's the hardest part— *that you'll always be here, but never in the way I want.*

Let Me Scream

Everyone else is flying, while I'm crawling on the
ground, and I can't help but wonder
Why I'm still here, spinning round. I want to be
more—to be better,to feel the wind beneath my feet,
but it's like I'm stuck in neutral, unable to find the
key to unlock this defeat. I'm not where I thought
I'd be, and the "me" I wanted to be feels like
someone else's dream, a goal that's too far to reach.
I want to run faster, faster than the days allow,
but the weight of my own expectations
keeps pulling me back somehow. will I ever feel like
I've arrived?or is this just the road I'll always travel,
Stumbling over every step I take, wondering if I'll
ever unravel the parts of me that feel stuck,
the pieces that don't seem to fit? will I ever be
enough in my own eyes—or is this just where I sit,
forever chasing a version of me
that's always a little bit out of reach?

Madison Farraway

On my 12th birthday, I felt 17.
On my 18th birthday, I felt 24.
I've lived a thousand different versions of my
adolescence in such a short time,
outgrowing myself, people, and hobbies before I
even knew what was worth keeping.

My mind wanders down those streets,
to places I've walked,
in every version of myself I could have been.
Sometimes, I still crave them.

but they always left me in holes—
I wake up from these daydreams,
reminiscing about those thousand versions I've
outgrown, still lingering in my thoughts, even now.
my stomach falls out of my body every time,
a reminder of what's been left behind.

Let Me Scream

She longed to feel something,
anything at all,
but mostly, she longed for you.

Madison Farraway

Here I stand, caught somewhere between the doors
of heaven and hell. For the first time in a lifetime,
I am unable to see where the light begins
and the darkness ends through this tunnel.

- *Uncertainty*

Let Me Scream

I am always in my head, not because I want to be, but because your distant memories are carved into my skin, stained into my brain, flooding through my veins, haunting me like a ghost that refuses to let go.

I am always in my head, not because I want to be, but because that is the only place I now find you.

- *Pieces of you*

Madison Farraway

They consumed every part of themselves that thrived on perfection, always wanting more. nothing was ever enough.

The addictive need to accomplish pushed them to set bigger and bigger goals, not to outdo others, but to outdo themselves. The pride from each success was fleeting, and once it passed, they were left needing more—more growth, more achievements, more validation. It was never truly about reaching the top, but the constant chase, the hunger for progress, and the satisfaction that was always just out of reach.

Let Me Scream

I watched you fall apart, piece by piece—
knowing what you had to do,
Your stomach was a weight, that weighed you down
your skin burned, your mind started to fog.
I watched your body break down, decay from the
outside-in, losing everything you once were.

Madison Farraway

She'd always tell me how good he was,
you see him on the outside,
I see him on the inside.
to be held,
to be loved by such a man,
to watch him grow and learn life,
to see him navigate it in ways that work best for
him. You see how good he is on the outside,
but he's double that on the inside.

Let Me Scream

I avoided the color purple for years,
like a child rejecting the clothes their parents had
laid out the night before.
I masked everything I was,
hiding the tenderness that lived within,
fearing that if I showed too much,
they would see me as less than.

I feared the way they might look at me with pity,
I shrank back,
dimming my own light,
thinking it safer to blend into the shadows.

Madison Farraway

She called her body a canvas,
using it to hold all her pain, while she burned within.
It was not hard to see, to the trained eye, that it was
a cry for help. She was begging for someone
to hold her the way she needed to be held.

You are untrained, and all of those signs were
unbeknownst to you.
You'd never know, and for that, you never will.
Maybe that is better, but she will forever be crying
for help, begging for you to read her.

Let Me Scream

You cannot put your life on pause for them,
as much as you'd like to,
It will slowly, but surely, make you lose yourself.
They are there to add to your life, not to be your life.
You can let them in when they're around,
but don't pause your life, hopelessly waiting for
them to be the person you need them to be.

Madison Farraway

You'd fall over and over again,
loving someone so emotionally unfulfilled,
trying to fill a void only they can heal themselves.
They took your love for weakness,
used it to their advantage,
and painted the narrative—
claiming to be the victim,
while you became the villain in their story.

Let Me Scream

Your whole world would stop when he stared and spoke to you, but it felt like he never truly listened. You'd watch as the spark slowly faded with every sigh, every dismissal, each time you questioned whether he could hear you for who you really were.

- *Until you burned out*

Madison Farraway

Coffee became energy drinks, I lived off temporary
energy and short-term dopamine,
scrolling, and liking over and over.

I stopped working out as much,
stopped prioritizing myself because your happiness
became more important than my own.

I had lost myself somewhere along the way,
I let myself go.

- *Somewhere in between now and then, your dreams became mine.*

Let Me Scream

I'd watch you as you grieved yourself,
your relationships, and the memories that failed to
follow through.

To grieve means you care,
It means you loved and yearned for something so
precious, something that slipped away or never truly
arrived.

Madison Farraway

How do you stand still when everything you've built, everything you've loved, feels like it could slip away at any moment? I feel disconnected—pulled away from myself, from everything I've known.

Falling in and out of love with people, with places, with who I am. Each day brings a new version of me, someone different, someone confused, searching for the pieces to put back together.

I fear that all of this—the good, the bad, the fleeting moments—will be ripped away without warning. And I will stand there once again, empty, wondering where I went wrong, searching for a sense of something I'll never be able to hold.

Let Me Scream

You savored every last drop of that beer,
It was sour, and you said "it didn't taste good,
but god, it felt good."
You loved how it made you feel,
the adrenaline, the rush—it consumed you.
I hated it, and you began to hate me for that.
Eventually, your disease latched onto me,
I was the dog, and you had the leash.
A chain I couldn't break, and a cycle that kept me
coming back to you.

Madison Farraway

That house haunts me, holding what could've been
behind, I'm always there, as if I never left,
trapped in the ghost of what could've been.
It gnaws at me, devours me,
slowly breaking me piece by piece.

   - *What could've been, but never was*

Let Me Scream

Home, a place to run from,
a place where hostility and drama were the only
ways to solve problems,
a place where instability became the norm,
an addiction to chaos that never lets you breathe.

I've longed to feel at home,
but I've become addicted to everything home wasn't
supposed to be.
Chasing the comfort of discomfort,
fighting for peace in a war that never ended.
I wanted a place to rest,
but instead, I became familiar with the storm.

Madison Farraway

You were a baby fed on grief,
consuming the remnants until you were no longer
hungry.

- *Generational trauma*

Let Me Scream

I need to move.
I need more, I need to move.
It feels empty, unsettling—
like my worth depends on it.
I need more,
I need to move.

I need more,
I'm starving.
I hunger for your validation so deeply
It's hard to give that to myself.
I'm still holding myself above water,
trying to convince myself that I'm enough for you.

Madison Farraway

She aches to be heard,
to feel truly seen, yearning for a love that always
danced beyond her grasp. There's a haunting beauty
in her longing, yet it lingers.

Let Me Scream

Love changes our perception of people,
making us overlook the bad,
convinced that the good is worth it.
We allow toxicity to seep in.

But what we need to understand
is that what we allow is what we get.
Toxicity doesn't begin in the relationship—
it starts with the relationship we have with
ourselves.

Madison Farraway

What is love?
Does it have boundaries,
with walls that rise,
carved with our pain?
It surrounds us,
slithers its way between us,
binding us with the weight of what we've suffered,
yet somehow, we still reach for it,
seeking warmth despite the distance.

Let Me Scream

I became a stranger to myself,
and I hated how it felt.
I lost touch with the things I once loved,
my days blending into one continuous loop,
a repetition of the last.

I grew a stranger to myself,
thinking that if I closed my eyes,
everything would fall back into place,
that I would somehow be led back to the pieces I
had lost along the way.
But I grew a stranger to myself,
not realizing the person I needed most
was standing right in front of me.

Madison Farraway

You cannot force someone to be who you need them
to be if it's not who they truly are.
Sometimes, the person you want most
is the one you're better off without.
Some things, some people, enter your life
but aren't meant to stay.
They teach you lessons,
leave imprint,
then you move onto the next chapter.

Find the strength to move on, to rebuild,
to grow beyond the need for them.

Let Me Scream

I mourn the girl I once was before you, before us,
but I also know I will spend the rest of my time,
drainingly translating myself, fully knowing that you
spoke my language.

- *The soft, gentle-spoken,
 innocent girl I was—until I wasn't.*

Madison Farraway

A hatred for myself, so calculated,
so rational, so carefully crafted.
It's a shadow that follows me relentlessly.
I feel dirty, weighed down by gloom. Dreading the hours ahead, fearing that this hatred will destroy the future I could have had.
It's easy to lose touch with the parts of yourself that once healed you—those parts fluent in the language of boundaries.

Let Me Scream

Love, it costs you your sense of direction,
leaving you lost.
Trying to navigate your way through it,
searching for a path you can't seem to find.

- *How love changed you*

Madison Farraway

I never realized how much I needed you
until now, as I sit, startled,
staring at the reflection of you in the mirror.
I question how I'd get by without you,
someone who watches me while I sleep,
holds me up in my lowest moments,
romanticizes the parts of me I hate,
someone who lifts me when I can't do it for myself,
who seeks me out in a crowded room,
who runs to me with news to share.

I look in the reflection of the mirror
and wonder how I ended up here,
how we ended up here,
and how I would manage
if he ever longed to feel more than me.

Let Me Scream

I slowly dismissed the walls I had so deeply buried
myself in, carefully disassembling them piece by
piece. I disregarded how much it would hurt
if I were ever without such a lovable soul.
I long to be loved the same.

Madison Farraway

You made it seem as though loving her was too difficult, She stares at the reflection of a broken soul, reliving every thought, every memory, a constant echo of what could have been.

Let Me Scream

I watched as you hungered,
emptied my plate to fill yours,
giving until there was nothing left to give.
A silent torture, full of invisible scars where the only
real evidence resides within.

- *The broken piece you neglected, and
  left for me to pick up*

Madison Farraway

Sometimes, it felt like the entire world had been lifted off my shoulders,
like I could breathe for the first time in a lifetime.
The weight of your body above mine,
I wanted to feel it for the rest of my days.
I wanted it to be you.
I wanted to feel.

    - *Longing*

Let Me Scream

I left the door unlocked,
mixing lust for love, attachment for obsession.
You cried, and I held you—
I thought this was trust,
I thought you'd light the match
and watch it twinkle in my eyes,
the ones you loved so passionately.

I grazed upon your skin,
mixing love for lust,
never knowing how to love
without leaving the doors wide open.

I left the windows unlocked too,
just in case you wanted to slither in.

Madison Farraway

Somehow, I turned your love into hate.
I grew sick of being loved through your filtered
words, each explanation leaving me empty.
longing to be consumed by your love,
but instead, it tore me apart.
My smile disappeared,
replaced by sleepless nights that couldn't hide the
ache. I forced a smile, as if pretending could make
you love me with the same intensity,
I tried to fix what was beyond fixing,
while you gave me distance when I needed love.

Let Me Scream

You want them to be the person they once were,
but as the image of them fades,
it's replaced by the person they are now.
You start to forget the softness, the love they gave—
until it's no longer there.

And you'll long to feel that person again,
because at one point,
they were everything you needed.

Madison Farraway

Nothing was better than something.
I'd rather have none of you than a fraction of what I
deserve. When you're gone, I'm gone too.
Maybe it wasn't me.
Maybe you just wanted somebody to hold,
somebody to love you in all the ways you need,
a reason to feel needed.

That void rots in me.
It gouges me, it holds me hostage.
The idea that we could be so full,
It breaks me.
It keeps me longing for something
we never quite had,
clinging to the illusion of what could have been.

Let Me Scream

She bottled up her feelings,
until regret became grief,
and love turned into hate.

She handed me her glass ,telling me to start
drinking. when she awoke,
she saw the mess she had made.

When love turns to despair, the consequences linger,
leaving behind the shattered pieces
of what once was.

Madison Farraway

That love turned into hate,
admiration warped into despair.
Chasing your perfection left a void within me,
a hollow I'll spend forever trying to mend.
It breaks me, consumes me— each thought, each
memory—until I'm nothing but the shadow
of who I thought I had to become.
Your perfection no longer holds me,
but now, as you find your interest, I lose mine.
It echoes endlessly in my mind,
a refrain that refuses to fade, refuses to release.

Let Me Scream

I started to fade, each letter of your name carved into
my chest, slowly replaced by shadows of doubt.
My mind twisted every memory,
fed on every fear,
until it devoured all that I was.

Madison Farraway

My heart grew cold and I lessened as a person.
The pain grew as I sought revenge,
the pieces of myself I lost in every soul I touched,
fearing I'd lose more with every exhale.

I wanted to drown out the flame between us,
losing fragments of who I was in the process.
I searched for you in everyone and everything,
forcing myself to let go,
when deep down, I wanted to hold on.

Let Me Scream

And I swallowed you, every piece of you.
I let you in, gave you a place to stay,
a place to cry, a spot to be.
I swallowed you, the bad parts too.
I abandoned myself in the process,

I would've jumped if you told me to.
Maybe that was the problem.
I lost myself in the hope that you'd find me,
In the spaces where I gave you all of me,
hoping you'd see the parts of me I left behind.
But I became so consumed with you,
I forgot to be whole without you.
And now I'm left,
with the pieces of me I traded away
for a love that never really saw me.

Madison Farraway

Finding Clarity Amidst Chaos

Chapter Three

In the midst of turmoil, there are fleeting moments of understanding—glimmers of clarity that guide us through the chaos. This chapter explores the journey of self-discovery in the face of life's uncertainties. Through introspection and resilience, the poems unravel the struggle to make sense of pain, loss, and confusion. It is within these chaotic moments that strength emerges, truths are uncovered, and clarity begins to take root.

Let Me Scream

I keep my gym bag in the back of my car,
filled with a collection of invisible scars.
I never know where I'll end up,

Maybe I've become a slave to your words,
a temporary fix for your fleeting need.
The scars that linger inside me
are far deeper than the ones you can see.
I carry this bag,
hoping, maybe one day,
somewhere will feel like home.

- *the weight of it all buried within*

Madison Farraway

They'll never understand.
You'll break and discard the pieces that are misread,
Shrinking, falling into a soul that's no longer yours.
You'll feed off the approval,
the constant need to be needed,
the endless hunger to be understood.
you'll carve a path of endless translation,
forever misunderstood.

Forever clinging to the hope that, just one day,
they will hear you.
That one day, they will feel the pain
that's been embedded so deep.
You'll shrink and fall,
molding yourself into someone they can love.

Let Me Scream

Sometimes, it is easier to grieve the things that once
were. Rather than work to overcome them,
we find ourselves in a vicious loop.
lingering in the past,
holding onto what slipped through our fingers,
afraid to move forward,
because the weight of what was is all we know.
We tell ourselves we're healing,
but healing is harder than remembering,
so we stay stuck, grieving the ghosts of a life that's
no longer ours to claim.

Madison Farraway

With every exhale, I felt pieces of myself slipping
away, a slow unraveling of the person I once was.
My mind drifts endlessly, trapped in the same
fractured memories,
each thought eroding the fragments of who I might
have been.

It's deafening—this invasive solitude.
To feel so utterly alone in a world teeming with life,
I almost believed I'd reached the depths of
emptiness.

Let Me Scream

I watched as you bled and bled,
every dream, every thought, slowly fading away.
I reassembled, removed, and built myself back,
attempting to give you the life you need to live
again.

Stuck in the spaces between hope and despair.
I tried to mend what was shattered,
only to realize some things can never be fixed,
some wounds too deep to heal.
And as I gave, I lost more of myself,
leaving pieces behind,
wondering if I'd ever be whole again.

Madison Farraway

That trauma sculpted and molded a path for hurt,
one that she would later claim as her identity.
It made relationships harder to love,
but easier to connect,
and much harder to understand.

She carved a path of pain and sorrow,
leaving herself disappointed,
lost in the echoes of being misunderstood.
The walls she built from her scars
became her protection and her prison,
separating her from the love she longed for

Let Me Scream

In order to love yourself,
in order to love who you are now,
you need to stop hating
the experiences that shaped you,
the moments that made the best of you,
the worst of you, and everything in between—
who you are today,
who you were yesterday,
and who you will be tomorrow.

Madison Farraway

Reminder:

You cannot force someone to love you in the ways you need to be loved,
nor can you make them understand a language they've never learned.

Let Me Scream

I woke up this morning with the same void I went to
sleep with, that hunger to be heard, to be
understood, it gnaws at me, relentless,
A hollow feeling that never fades.

That void consumes me,
it breaks me piece by piece,
a constant reminder of what I long for,
yet never seem to find.

Madison Farraway

Contentment—to know, to feel, to be ingrained into
my soul, to think, to feel, to be so okay in this skin
that rests along my bones.
To grieve the childhood lost along the way,
to love, then to hate—the short-lived feeling of
being content.

There will never be enough life for me,
so much to be, to know, to live.
There is not enough time to be everything I need to
be—for myself, for him, for her,
for that little girl who still rests dormant within.

How could I ever be enough for you,
if I couldn't ever be enough for myself?
How could I ever love you fully,
if I can't even give myself the love I need to grow?
How can I be enough for you,
if I'm not enough for myself? Time—the endless
chase, always slipping away before I can catch up to
who I am, who I could be.

Let Me Scream

She'd always hoped to feel at home,
a place she wasn't sure existed in this lifetime.
A place where contentment lived,
a place she wouldn't have to run from,
a place where she felt whole.

Longing for a home that never was,
a sanctuary she couldn't find,
a place where her heart could rest,
where love didn't feel like a fight,
where the weight of the world wasn't always on her shoulders.

She searched for that peace,
but it always felt just out of reach,
a dream she could never hold,
a hope she clung to in the silence.

Madison Farraway

If they cared, they'd be here,
they wouldn't have done what they did.
someone who loves you would value you,
and hold you when things get tough.
They wouldn't run to other arms,
they wouldn't search for someone else.
A person who truly loves you, would stay.

Let Me Scream

And after all of this,
you'll find yourself.
You'll heal.
You'll discover parts of you that were lost,
and you'll learn yourself in ways you couldn't have
with them. Through the pain, you'll grow stronger.
You'll reclaim what was always yours.
And in time, you'll become who you were meant to
be.

Madison Farraway

The more you forgave them,
the more they hurt you.
The more you forgave,
the more they saw your love as weakness.
they knew you wouldn't leave,
so they kept taking,
Turning your kindness into a tool for destruction.
Until you were nothing but a ghost of the person you once were, a statue of the potential you could've been.

Let Me Scream

You lied to me, so much that I think you started
believing your own lies.
I let the storm pass,
knowing a rainbow would follow.
The next storm would come,
but once it passed,
I'd leave it behind—
forgetting, as I should,
the past where it belongs.

Madison Farraway

Why would you regret the experiences that shaped you into who you are today?
You disregard the growth that comes with every struggle, every lesson learned.
Own your life, because it's yours to write.
Every mistake, every triumph, is a part of your story.
Don't erase the chapters that made you stronger,
for *they're the foundation of who you're becoming.*

Let Me Scream

Loneliness will creep upon you,
late at night,
as memories slip under the sheets with you.
Let this be your reminder that you're free.
Don't disregard the bad just to hold on to the good.
The loneliness will fade, and you will heal.

Madison Farraway

Reminder:

<u>Unconditional love does not mean staying when you know you should leave.</u>

Let Me Scream

Don't neglect the parts of you that are begging to be
loved. Let yourself feel, even the pain,
because in embracing it,
you'll find healing.

Give yourself permission to be whole,
to exist fully—
both the broken and the beautiful parts

Madison Farraway

Stop breaking your heart
trying to be the person they want you to be.
Instead, be the person you need to be for yourself,
because you're worth more than
surrounding yourself in places where you're not
valued.

Let Me Scream

At what cost did it take you to get here?
How many pieces of yourself did you lose,
fighting battles no one ever saw?

You wore armor,
but I wonder, did it ever protect you from the things
you could not speak? From the silent tears that fell
When no one was looking?

Madison Farraway

I lit my regret,
reclaimed the pieces I left behind in the things I used
to love, but grew to hate.
Each fragment flickered in the flame,
whispering memories of who I was,
only to be swallowed by the fire
that warmed the void inside me.

I kept holding on,
even as the smoke twisted into shapes
I didn't recognize,
searching for something
to make it all worth the burn.

Let Me Scream

Somewhere between loving you and hating you,
I forgot how to love myself.
I forgot how to talk, how to smile,
I lost who I was—or who I could be without you.
I was unhappy without you,
convinced that maybe I needed you.
but what I really needed was to be needed by
myself. I needed to find myself again.

Madison Farraway

You are allowed to speak
about what they did and how it hurt you.
You are allowed to grieve and to hurt.
You are allowed to cry,
to take up space,
to scream and shout.

Don't worry about being a burden,
because the people who truly care
will sit with you until you're ready to let go.
That is love, that is what you do for the people you
love. And sometimes, all you need
is to know someone is there.

Let Me Scream

If they loved you,
they wouldn't have left you wondering where you fit
into their life.
They wouldn't have left you begging for their love,
because the people who truly love you
would never leave you questioning why they
couldn't have been better.

- *The people who love you make sure you know*

Madison Farraway

Stop perceiving them as someone they are not,
stop idealizing them into something they're not,
stop excusing their bad habits as mistakes.

- *let them be the person they show you,
 not the one you wish them to be*

Let Me Scream

They cannot value you,
they do not take the time to learn beyond what can
be seen on the surface.
To love unconditionally is to love whole,
every imperfection and every perfection.

Madison Farraway

If they truly cared,
change would have come by now.

you wouldn't have to wait for the call.
they'd be right there beside you.

- *Somethings aren't fair*

Let Me Scream

There are moments when the truth feels too heavy,
so the mask slips on, and the walls grow higher.
Behind closed doors, a reflection stares back—
lost, broken, untouched by the light.
In those quiet moments,
it seems easier to be someone else,
to wear a face that's not quite yours.
As if the world outside couldn't see through
the layers you've built.
But in the silence,
the weight of it all is still there,
unspoken and unanswered.

Madison Farraway

Sometimes, home isn't a person,
but the places where you had to lose yourself
to find the better parts of who you are.

- *The moments when you had to pick yourself
  up and learn to stand again.*

Let Me Scream

There is no such thing as too many "I love you's"
no such thing as too many compliments,
too many hugs, kisses, or laughs.
But there is such a thing as not enough.

If you love, love wholeheartedly.

Madison Farraway

Compliment them.
Tell them the things you love about them—
a friend, a partner, or a stranger.
Hold the people you care about close,
and make sure they know how deeply you love
them. There's no such thing as too much love.
Don't shrink yourself to fit the expectations of
small-minded people; be more.

Let Me Scream

Get comfortable with being alone. Sit with uncomfortable feelings. Learn to find contentment within yourself. Grow to be happy in your own presence, so you're not relying on someone else to fill a void that only you can fill.

- *Sometimes, you have to get lost,
  so you can find yourself again*

Madison Farraway

You knew you loved them
the moment you stayed,
even when you knew you should've left.

Let Me Scream

I need it all, I need it all out,
to be met with something—anything—
but the silence is deafening.
I feel myself slipping as the silence gets louder
that the space between us is growing and something
is fading that I can't quite grasp but I sit here
relearning the same painful lessons, as if I've never
learned from the last.

Madison Farraway

Beneath it all, she's still the same broken girl she was ten years ago. She's searching for something, anything, to ease this constant feeling of uncertainty— a lack of clarity, a direction she always seems to see but can never quite reach. Her mind is loud, and invasive, constantly drowning in endless thoughts.
Chasing answers but only finds more questions, caught in a cycle she can't escape.
She wonders if there's something outside of herself that can fix it—moving away from everything she once so deeply loved, making new connections, new mistakes—but deep down, knowing it's not about changing what is around but maybe starting with herself.

- *To find peace in a storm that never ends*

Let Me Scream

Let me scream—
to be heard, to release the weight
that crushed my chest, my voice, my will.
Let me shatter the silence
with every jagged piece of myself,
spilling the truth I buried too deep.

Let me scream for the nights I was unheard,
for the moments I swallowed the pain whole,
and for the love that turned to ashes in my hands.
Let me scream for the me that still lingers,
clinging to what could have been,
aching for what will never return.

Let me scream—
a final act of defiance,
a reclamation of everything stolen,
and a release of what I no longer need.

    - *Letting go*

www.ingramcontent.com/pod-product-compliance
Lightning Source LLC
Chambersburg PA
CBHW072211070526
44585CB00015B/1295